Down by the sea

Story by Joan Jarden   Illustrations by Susy Boyer Rigby

Meg's grandma had a house by the sea.

"Look, Meg!" said Grandma.
"The waves are little today.
I can take you to see
the rock pools."

"Oh, good!" said Meg.

Meg and her grandma
went for a walk on the rocks.

They looked inside the rock pools.
Grandma saw some baby shells.
Meg saw some little black fish.

A big boat went by.

Meg and Grandma
did not see the big boat.

They did not see the big wave
that it made.

Meg looked down into a little pool.
"That shell is going for a walk!"
she said.

"A crab is inside it," said Grandma.
"It's a hermit crab.
Can you see its legs?"

Then Grandma looked up.

She saw the big wave coming!

"Meg!" she shouted.

"Look out!"

The big wave from the boat splashed down on the rocks. It splashed all over Grandma's legs, but **Meg** did not get wet.

Meg and Grandma
laughed and laughed.

"Oh Grandma, you are all wet," said Meg.
"I will have to take you home!"